AF614133

Janusz Meyerhoff

Mysterious Megalithic Structures

First Edition 2013
ISBN 978-1-304-64677-4

Index

Foreword

Definition.
Megalithic means "large stone", this word is used to refer to any huge human build or assembled structure or collection of stones or boulders. They were built between about 8,000 and 4,000 years ago in Europe, during the Neolithic and Bronze ages.
People.
Long time before the Indo-European tribes arrived in Europe and parts of Asia people were already living there, as well everywhere in the world. The builders were Neolithic, primitive farmers and herders of cattle, sheep and goats. Not much is known about them they only left strange monolithic monuments of: stone, wood, or earth. To build such enormous megalithic structure cooperation between members of community is a must. Also, somebody who decides what, where and when the megalithic structure will be built? Some sort of hierarchy was essential.

Why they were built?
Some of the uses were: elite burials, mass burials, meeting places, astronomical observatories, religious centers, temples, shrines, processional lanes, territory markers, status symbols. However, its use can never be known for sure. They may have had multiple functions because they were used by different cultural groups over the millennia. Also, few retain their original configuration, having been eroded or vandalized or simply modified.

Types of Megalithic Structures

* Following is a list of megalithic monuments:

* Cairns, mounds, kurgans, barrows, kofun, stupa, tope, tumuli: all these different names for man-made hills of earth or stone.

* Dolmens, cromlechs, obelisks, menhir: single large standing stones.

* Woodhenges: a structure made of concentric circles of wooden posts.

* Stone circles, cycloliths: a circular monument made of free standing stones.

* Henges: a parallel ditch and bank pattern of construction, circular in shape.

* Recumbent stone circles: Two vertical stones, one horizontal placed between them, to watch the moon as it slides along the horizon.

* Passage tombs, shaft tombs, chambered tombs, tholos tombs: Architectural buildings of shaped or cut stones, containing burials and covered with earthen mound.

* Quoits: two or more stone slabs with a capstone, sometimes representing a burial.

* Stone rows: linear path made by placing two rows of stones on both sides of a straight pathway.

* Cursus: linear feature made by two ditches and two banks, strait or with doglegs.

* Stone cists, stone boxes: small square boxes made of stones which contain human bones.

* Fogou, souterrains, fuggy holes: underground passages with stone walls.

* Chalk giants: a type of geoglyph, images carved into the white chalk hillside.

The following texts will be dedicated to different, megalithic constructions around the world. The first will be Stonehenge, for the simple reason that its investigation took many years and it is the best known monolithic monument.

Stonehenge

Stonehenge is a prehistoric monument in Wiltshire, England, about 3 km west of Amesbury and 13 km north of Salisbury, One of the most famous sites in the world. It is in the densest complex of Neolithic and Bronze Age monuments in England, including several hundred burial mounts.

Stonehenge

Before 8,000 BC

Stonehenge was a prehistoric structure consisting of a ring of standing stones set within earthworks. It is in the middle of the densest complex of Neolithic and Bronze Age monuments in England, including several hundred burial mounds.

Stonehenge evolved in several constructions phases spanning at least 1,500 years.

Four or five, large Mesolithic postholes, which date around 8,000 BC, had been found beneath the modern car-park. These pine posts were around 0.75 meters in diameters. Three or possibly four were in an east-west alignment which had ritual significance. Similar sites have been found in Scandinavia.

The date 8,000 BC has a special significance. It was a time when the last glacial period ended. The ice sheet which covered England, Ireland and part of northern Europe was melting and then the forests started to grow. These trees from which postholes were made were from these forests.

But, who were the people who erected these posts? Two possibilities exist:

1. They survived the harsh condition of glacial period in England.
2. They came from elsewhere, probably from south, where the conditions, during the last glacial period, were better.

Stonehenge 1 - ca. 3,100 BC.

The first structure consisted of a circular bank and ditch enclosure made of Seaford Chalk, measuring about 110 meters in diameter, with a large entrance to the north-east and a smaller one to the south. The builders placed the bones of deer and oxen at the bottom of the ditch. After 3,100 BC the ditch began to silt up naturally. Within the outer edge of the enclosed area is a circle of 56 pits, each about a meter in diameter, known as the Aubrey holes after John Aubrey, the 17th century antiquarian who identify them.

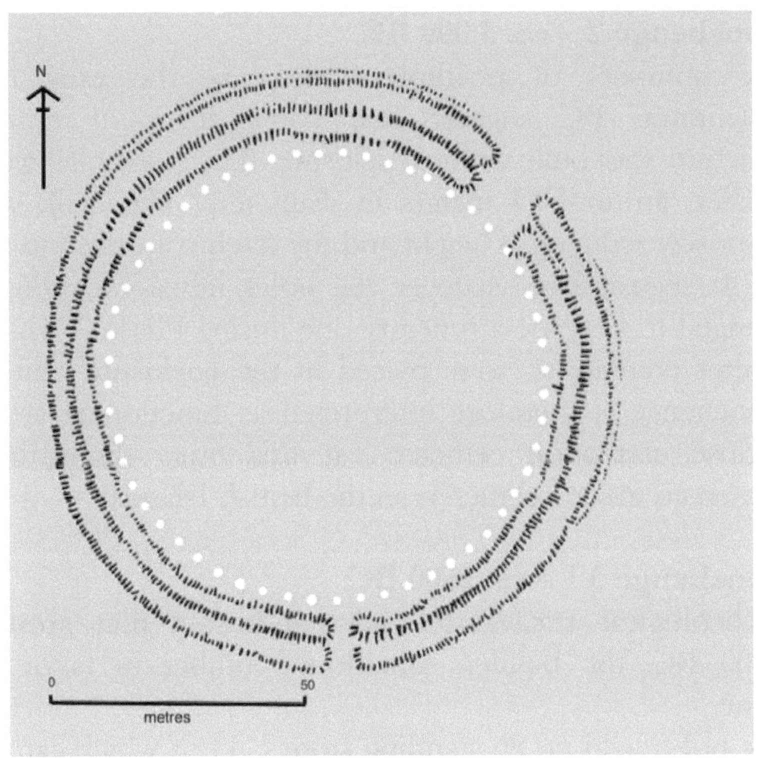

Stonehenge

In 2013 a team of archeologists, led by Professor Parker Pearson, excavated more than 50,000 cremated bones of 63 individuals buried at Stonehenge. Radiocarbon dating of the remains has put the date of the site 500 years earlier than previously estimated, to around 3,000 BC. Physical and chemical analysis of the remains has shown that cremations were almost equal between men and women and children.

Analysis of animal teeth suggests that as many as 4,000 people gathered at the side for the mid-winter and mid-summer festivals. Some people traveled from as far as the Scottish Highlands for the celebration. At that time, the whole world was scarcely populated (4 or 5 million people). Those were immense meetings!

Stonehenge 2 – ca. 3,000 BC.

The numbers of postholes dating to the early 3rd millennium BC suggest that some form of timber structure was built within enclosure. The postholes were smaller, around 0.4 meters in diameters. The bank was purposely reduced in height and the ditch continued to silt up. It seems that whatever the holes initial function, it changed to become a funerary one during Phase 2. Thirty further cremations were placed in the enclosure's ditch. Stonehenge is therefore interpreted as functioning as an enclose cremation cemetery, at this time, the earliest known cremation cemetery in the British Islands.

Stonehenge 3 I – ca. 2600 BC.

Archeological excavations have indicated that around 2,600 BC, the builders abandoned timber in favor of stone.

The holes held up 80 standing stones, 43 of which can be traced today. Other standing stones were small Sarsens, used later as lintels. The stones, which weighted about four tones, were made from around 20 different types of rock.

The north-eastern entrance was widened; it precisely matched the direction of mid-summer sunrise and mid-winter sunset of the period.

The Heelstone was erected outside the north-eastern entrance. Two or three, large portal stones were set up inside the north-eastern entrance. Stonehenge Avenue, a parallel pair of ditches and banks leading 3 kilometers to the River Avon, was also added.

Stonehenge 3 II – 2600 BC to 2400 BC.

30 enormous **Sarsen** stones were brought to the site. They came from a quarry, around 40 kilometers north of Stonehenge. The stones were erected as a 33 meters diameters circle of standing stones, with a ring of 30 lintel stones on top. The lintels were fitted to one another using woodworking technique. Each standing stone was around 4.1 meters high, 2.1 meters wide and weighted around 25 tones. The lintel stones are around 3.2 meters long, 1 meter wide and 0.8 meters thick.

Within this circle stood five trilithons arranged in a horseshoe shape 13.7 meters across and facing north east. They were linked using complex jointing.

The image of a dagger and of 14 axe heads have been carved on one of the sarsens; dated to the late Bronze Age.

The pair of trilithons in the north-east is smallest (6 meters high) and the largest in south-west of the horseshoe stone is 7.5 meters high.

At about the same time, a large timber circle and a second avenue were constructed 3.2 kilometers away at Durrigton Walls overlooking the River Avon. The timber circle was oriented towards the rising sun on the midwinter solstice, opposing the solar alignment at Stonehenge, whilst the avenue was aligned with the setting sun.

The two avenues and both circles were connected; they were used as a procession route on the longest and shortest days of the year.

Stonehenge 3 IV – 2280 BC to 1930 BC.

Only minor changes were made in this phase. The blue stones were arranged in a circle between the two rings of Sarcens and in an oval at the center of the inner ring. Some of these bluestones were from a second group brought from Wales. The Altar stone have been moved within the oval and re-erected vertically. Stonehenge 3 IV was shabbily built compared to its predecessors – newly re-installed bluestones were not well founded and began to fall over.

Stonehenge 3 V - 1930 BC to 1600 BC.

Soon afterwards, the north eastern section of the phase 3 IV bluestone circle was removed, creating a horseshoe-shaped setting which mirrored the shape of the central sarsen trilithons.

After 1600 BC.

After 1600 BC the use of Stonehenge ended. This site was known to scholars since the Middle Ages and since then it has been studied by numerous groups.

Ötzi

Of course, Ötzi was not a megalithic monument, but it is a perfectly preserved natural mummy of a man who lived about 3.300 BC (age of Megalithic structure). The mummy was found in September 1991 in the Otztal Alps, on the border between Austria and Italy. He is Europe's oldest natural human mummy and has offered an unprecedented view of ancient Europeans.

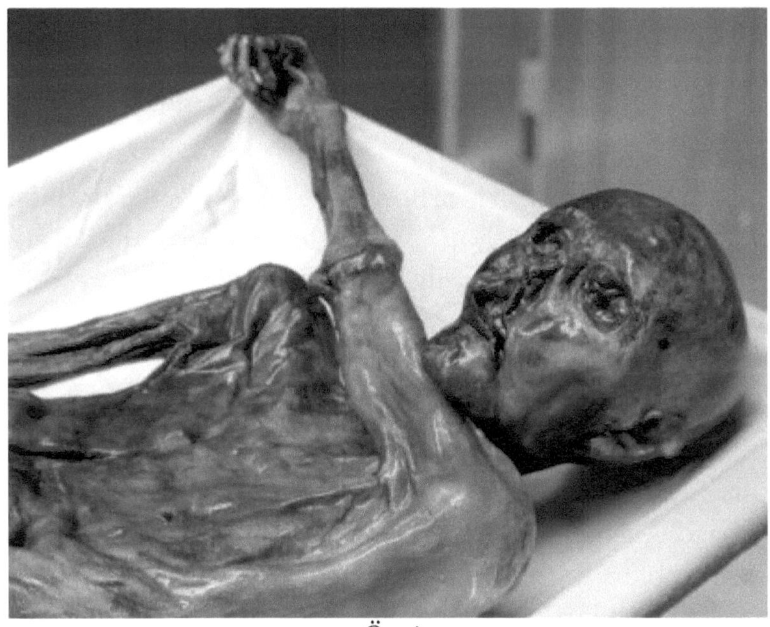

Ötzi

Body.

Ötzi was approximately 1.65 meters tall, weighted about 50 kilograms and was about 45 years of age. Analysis of

pollen, dust grains and tooth enamel indicates that he spent his childhood near the present day village of Feldthurns, north of Bolzano, but later went to live in valleys 50 kilometers further north.
Analysis of Ötzi's intestinal contents showed two meals, the last one eight hours before his death, one of chamois meat, and the other of red deer. Both were eaten with grain, roots and fruits. In the proximity of the body, and thus originating from Ötzi provisions, were chaff and grains of einkorn, barley, seeds of flax and poppy and various seeds of berries growing in the wild were discovered.
Pollens of wheat and legumes shows that they were domesticated crops.
High levels of both: copper particles and arsenic were found in Ötzi's hair. Also copper axe which is 99.7 % pure copper indicates that Ötzi was involved in copper smelting.
By examining the proportion of Ötzi's tibia, femur and pelvis, Christopher Ruff has determined that Ötzi's lifestyle included long walks over hilly terrain – could be that Ötzi was a high-altitude shepherd.

Health.

Ötzi had whipworm, an intestinal parasite. Three or four of his right ribs had been cracked after death, or when the ice had crushed his body. Otzi's teeth showed considerable internal deterioration from cavities – he eat grain-heavy, high carbohydrate diet. Otzi was also lactose intolerant.

Tattoos.

Ötzi had several carbon tattoos including groups of short, parallel, vertical lines to both sides of the lumbar spine and various marks around both ankles. Radiological examination of his bones showed "age-condition or strain-induced degeneration" in these areas, including osteochondrosis and slight spondylosis in the lumbar spine and degeneration in the knee and ankle joints. Maybe, that these tattoos have been related to pain relief treatments similar to acupressure and acupuncture. If so this is at least 2000 years before its earliest use in China.

Clothes and shoes.

Ötzi's clothes were sophisticated. He wore a cloak made of woven grass and a coat, a belt, a pair of leggings, a loincloth and shoes, all made of leather of different skins He also wore a bearskin cap with a leather chin strap. The shoes were waterproof and wide, prepared for walking across the snow. They were made from bearskin for the soles, deer hide for the top panels and netting made of tree bark. Soft grass went around the foot which functioned like modern socks. The coat, belt, leggings and loincloth were constructed of vertical strips of leather sewn together with sinew. His belt had a pouch sewn to it that contained a cache of useful objects: a scrapper, drill, flint flake, bone awl and dried fungus.

The shoes were so complex that even 5.300 years ago, people had the equivalent of a cobbler who made shoes for other people.

Tools and equipment.

Other items found with Ötzi were a copper axe with a wood handle, a flit-bladed knife with an ash handle, and a quiver of 14 arrows. Two of the arrows were broken and were tipped with flint and had fletching (stabilizing fins).

12 remaining were not finished and untipped. The arrows were found in a quiver with a bow string and antler tool for sharpening arrow points.

Ötzi´s flint knife and sheath

In addition, among Ötzi's possessions were berries, two birch bark baskets, and two species of polypore mushroom with leather strings through them. One of these, Birch fungus has antibacterial properties while the other "tinder fungus", included part of a complex fire-starting kit.

Ötzi's copper axe head, 9.5 centimeters long, is made of almost pure copper, and the haft is 60 centimeters long, made from wood.
At that time, such an axe would have been a valuable possession, important as a tool and as a "status Symbols".

Ötzi's death.

X-rays and a scan revealed that Ötzi had an arrowhead lodged in his left shoulder when he died, and a matching small tear on his coat. This discovery prompted the researches to theorize that Ötzi died from blood loss. However farther research found the arrow's shaft had been removed before death, an examination of the body found bruises, cuts to the hand, wrists and chest and cerebral trauma indicative to a blow the head. Researches are unsure what a cause of his death was: blood loss caused by an arrow, blow to the head, or being struck by a rock by another person.

Ötzi gave us invaluable information's about the life of these ancient people. They were much more sophisticated and technologically advanced that we ever thought. He lived at a time when megalithic structures were built – did he participated in constructions or religious ceremonies which usually were performed near or inside these megalithic monuments? – Probably, but it will never be known!

Megalithic Structures in Malta

The Megalithic Temples in Malta and a small island, Gozo are located in the Mediterranean Sea off the south coast of Sicily. The temples are among the oldest in the word 2000 to 4000 BC. In all, there are 30 temples on Malta and Gozo and there may have been **more**. They were also built throughout Sicily, Italy and central Mediterranean.

Pre-temple Period (5500 – 4500 BC).

Malta and Gozo were first colonized about 5500 BC, by people from the Neolithic cultures from Sicily, the nearest landmass. The pre-temple economy was based on agriculture: wheat, barley, horticulture, and herding: sheep, goats, cattle, and pigs. The original settlements were small clusters of huts build from of wattle and daub. At this point, Malta and Gozo shared symbols and institutions with Sicily and southern Italy, suggesting trade contacts. Stone axes and obsidian were traded to the islands.

Skorba Phase (4500- 4100 BC).

During the Skorba Phase on Malta and Gozo, the population increased on the islands and the construction of larger and more villages continued. The cultural connection with Italy, Sicily, and Central Mediterranean increased. Also a consolidation of agricultural production led to the beginning of social stratification.

Communal structures (ritual) were first built during the Skorba Phase, but they were small and for general purpose only.

Zebbug Phase (4100 – 3800 BC).
The Zebbug Phase brought new, distinct pottery styles, similar to those made in Sicily.

Megalithic temples.
They were low, sprawling stone structure with between 5 and 20 rooms. Each temple was enclosed within a massive retaining wall and forecourts for public gathering. The internal courtyard was leading to the private rooms The Malta temples are entirely curvilinear, consisting of a series of lobed spaces. The earliest temples were simple, made of two or three oval rooms. But, the later ones, after a thousand years of use, were massive and sprawling.

Doorway

The doorways into the temple were monumental; they were boundaries marking the interior (private) and exterior (public) parts of the temples. These separations were also market by raised thresholds and stone paved floors.

The outer walls of the temples formed a semi-circular forecourt to the south, paved with crushed limestone blocks.

In some cases, the walls were double and the space inside is filled with rubble. Some of the entrances points to the southeast - perhaps, meeting the rising sun.

Internal Structures.

The dark interiors of the Malta Temples suggest that the temples have originates as above-ground replication of rock-cut tombs. Several of the complex temples are associated with the mega burial sites; but the temples themselves do not contain burials. When the roofs were intact, they were dark, enclosed space, with red-plastered walls, labyrinthine, dark passages which had eerie acoustical properties. The buildings are too massive for the needs of population.

Interior of the Temple

The temples have a different inside and outside, a division between front and rear. Access to the interior is restricted by way of a series of doorways and closed off areas. In some temple are "oracle holes" narrow slots in the wall which connect the inner temples with exterior rooms.
The inner furniture consist of built-in stones tables or "altars" and stone doors. Artifacts found inside the temples include: obsidian tools, polished stone axes, amulets, pottery, and small figurines of females without clearly defined sexual attributes. Animal sacrifices inside the temples were performed because a number of animal bones, and flint blades were found.

Archeological Excavations

The ruins have been recognized, long time before, during the 16th century. But first archeological systematic work on the temples was conducted by John D. Evans in 1950.
Only two excavations in Malta and none in Gozo were made, but they showed that the people on Malta and Gozo lived in small oval or round huts build of stone and daub, requiring frequent rebuilding. In comparison, the temples were massive, visually prominent and took lots of work to build them.

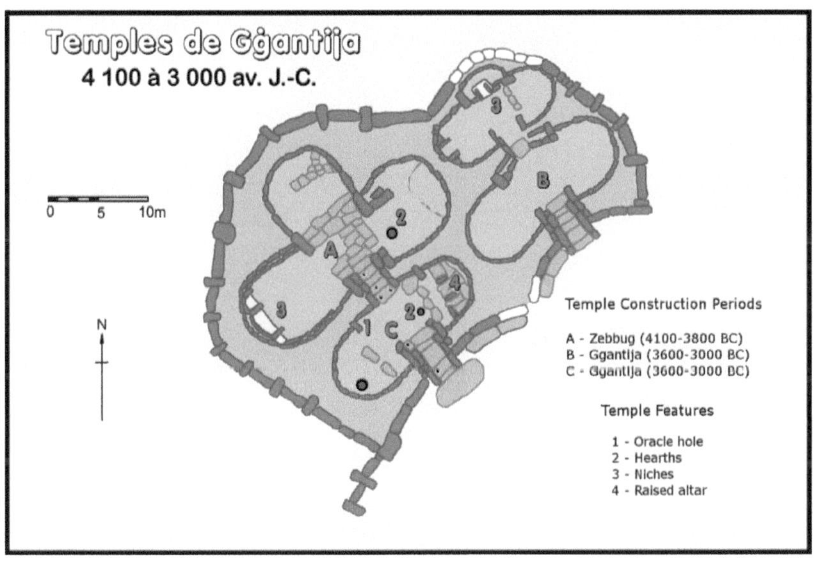
Temples de Gġantija
4 100 à 3 000 av. J.-C.
0 5 10m
N
Temple Construction Periods
A - Zebbug (4100-3800 BC)
B - Ggantija (3600-3000 BC)
C - Ggantija (3600-3000 BC)
Temple Features
1 - Oracle hole
2 - Hearths
3 - Niches
4 - Raised altar

Megalithic Structure in Orkney

Orkney is an archipelago of 70 islands of which 20 are inhabited in northern Scotland, about 16 kilometers north of the coast of Caithness. There are numerous prehistoric remains in Orkney; four of them form a World Heritage Site.

There are various reasons for the abundance of archeological sites. The sandstone provides easily workable stone material and the wind-blown sand helped preserve these ancient structure.

Of course, not all archeological sites will be described, due to the abundance of sites, most important only.

Early history.

About 4000 BC the worldwide sea level was much lower, so Orkney Islands were attached to the northern Scotland. Also, there are indications that the islands were already occupied by Neolithic nomadic tribes by approximately 6700 BC.

Knap of Howar.

The earliest known permanent settlement is "Knap of Howar", on the island "Papa Westrey", the farmstead consist of two adjacent rounded rectangular thick-walled buildings with low doorways linked by a passageway. The structure was inhabited from 3700 BC to 2600 BC but probably it was built on a side of even older settlement. Unstan ware pottery was found on the site, which was discovered in the 1920s when the gale exposed the coastline.

Knap of Howar

Barnhouse Settlements.

The second oldest is "Barnhouse Settlement", a cluster of fifteen buildings, occupied between 3200 – 2950 BC. (Its 800 years before the Egyptian were building pyramids) The houses were built above ground level, and included, recessed box beds, a central hearth, and stone dresser. There is also a network of stone drains leading to a common ditch. Potteries, flints, flakes of pitchstone have been found on this side.

Barnhouse

Skara Brae.

The third oldest is "Skara Brae", occupied between 3100 – 2500 BC, consisting of ten clustered houses, similar to those at Barnhouse, but they are linked by a common passage to a room containing ash, bones, stones and organic waste. Only the roofs, which were supported by timber or whalebones, were visible from the outside. A variety of bone beads, pins, pendants and four carved stone balls were also found in this side.

Skara Brae

Maeshowe.

The Maeshowe, dated about 3000 BC, is a large chambered cairn and passage grave. "Howe" is an element in a name, from the Old Norse word "haugr" meaning mound or barrow, common throughout Orkney. The grass mound hides a complex of passages and chambers build of crafted slabs of sandstones. It is aligned so that the rear wall of its central chamber, a cube of 4.5 cubic meters, is illuminated on the winter solstice.

After it was abandoned during the Bronzer Age, Maeshowe was used by Vikings from 9th to the 12 century AD which left many runic inscriptions on stone walls. Also crusaders in the winter of 1153 AD left some inscriptions. Over thirty inscriptions remain the largest collection in Europe.

Maeshow

Ring of Brodgar.

The Ring of Brodgar is a henge and stone circle 104 meters in diameters, originally made of 60 stones, of which 27 remain. It is set within a circular ditch 3 meters deep and 10 meters wide. It is estimated that the ditch alone took 80.000 man-hours to construct. The ring stands on a small isthmus between the Lochs of Stenness and Harray. It has been erected between 2500 BC and 2000 BC. The excavations at the Ness of Brodgar site and the Ring of Stenness have revealed several buildings: ritual and domestic. One structure is 20 meters long by 11 meters wide. Pottery, bones, stone tools and polished stone mace heads have also been discovered. The most important find is the remains of a large stone wall 100 meters long and 4 meters wide, which traverse the entire peninsula.

Also a rock colored red, orange and yellow was found. The paint has been made by mixing iron ore with animal fat, milk or eggs. It is evidence that Neolithic people used paint to decorate their buildings.

Ring of Broadgard

Stones of Stenness.

The stones of Stenness are fife remaining megalith of a henge, the largest is 6 meters high. The site dates around 3100 BC. The stones are part of a landscape that had ritual significance for the "Grooved ware people". The Ring of Brodgar lies about 1.2 kilometers to the north, Maeshowe the same distance to the east, and Barnhouse is only 150 meters to the north.

The existing megaliths were part of an elliptical shaped stone circle of 12 stones, about 32 meters in diameters surrounded by a ditch that was 2 meters wide and 7 meter deep and with a single entrance causeway on the north that faces towards the Barnhouse Settlement. The Watch Stone stands outside the circle to the north-west and is 5.6 meters high. Other smaller stones include a square stone like a huge hearth setting in the centre of the circle. Bones of cattle, sheep, wolves and dogs were found in the ditch, what suggest ritual sacrifice and feasting.

Stones of Stenness

Dwarfie Stane.

The Dwarfie Stane tomb on the island of Hoy is made from a single huge block of red sandstone with a hollowed-out central chamber. This style is quiet unlike any other Neolithic Orkney Megalithic structure. This site is around 2500 BC old.

Dwarfie Stane

Megalithic Structure in Brittany, France

Near the French village of Carnac, in Brittany is an exceptionally dense collection of megalithic sites, consisting of alignments, dolmens, tumuli and single menhirs. More than 3,000 prehistoric standing stones were made from local rock. It's the largest collection in the world. Most of megalithic stones are inside the village of Carnac, but some are within the village of La Trinite-sur-Mer. Most of the stones were erected during the Neolithic period, around 3,300 BC, but some are amazingly old, 4,500 BC.

Of course, not all Megalithic structure in Brittany could be described, few of them only.

Menec alignments.

Eleven converging rows of menhirs stretching for 1,165 by 100 meters are the remains of stone circles. A cromlech containing 71 stone blocks is at western part and a very ruined cromlech at the eastern end. The largest stones around 4 meters high, are at the wider, western end, then becoming smaller, 0.6 meters high along the length of the alignment before growing in heights toward the extreme eastern end.

Menec alignments

Kermario alignments.

The Kermario (House of the Dead) alignments consist of 1029 stones in ten columns, about 1,300 meters long. However, aerial photography has revealed a stone circle in the eastern part, where the stones are smaller.

Kermario alignments

Kerlescan alignments.
To the east, of the others two alignments, is a group of 555 stones consisting of 13 lines with a total length of about 800 meters. The stones vary in height from 80 centimeters to 4 meters. At the extreme west, where the stones were tallest, there is a stone circle of 39 stones. It is also possible that another circle existed in the northern part.

Kerlescan alignments

Menec, Kermario and Kerlescan alignments may have once formed a single, much bigger group, that have been divided and the stones were used for other purposes.

Tumuli.
There are several tumuli, mounds of earth, build over the grave. They usually are a passage leading to a central chamber which originally held Neolithic objects.

Tumuli Saint-Michael.

The tumulus of Saint-Michael was constructed between 5.000 BC and 3.400 BC. The tumulus is 125 meters long, 60 meters wide and 12 meters high. To build it was necessary to use 35.000 cubic meters of stone and earth. It was a tomb of a ruling class and contained various funerary objects: 15 stone chests, pottery and jewels.

A chapel was built on top of tumuli in 1663 and it was reconstructed on various occasions.

Tumuli Saint-Michael

Tumuli Moustoir.

The tumulus Moustoir, also known as "El Mane", is a chamber tomb 85 meters long, 35 meters wide and 5 meters high. A dolmen stands at the west end and two tombs at the east end. Nearby is a small menhir, approximately 3 meters high.

Dolmens.

There are several dolmens scattered around the area, which are considered to have been tombs. However, the acid soil of surrounding area eroded the bones. The dolmens were constructed of several large stones supporting a capstone. Originally buried under the mound of earth, however due to archeological excavations the mound has been removed and only large stones remain. Also natural causes, like persistent rain could have eroded the mound.

Dolmen Er-Roch-Feutet.

To the north and near the Chapelle de la Madelaine is located dolmen Er-Roch-Feutet, which has a totally covered roof.

Dolmen Er-Roch-Feutet

Dolmen Kercado.

A rare dolmen covered by its original cairn. It is placed south of the Kermario alignment and is 25 to 30 meters wide and 5 meters high. On top it has a small menhir and is surrounded by a circle of small, 4 meters high menhirs. The main passage is 6,5 meters long and leads to a large chamber where many objects were found: axes, pearls, arrow heads and pottery. It was constructed around 4,600 BC and used for almost 1,600 years.

Dolmen Crucuno.

A Crucuno dolmen has a 40 ton table-stone resting on pillars around 1.8 meters high. Before 1900, it was connected by a passage 24 meters long.

Dolmen Crucuno

Dolmen "La Madeleine".

A large dolmen, 12 by 5 meters, on the top is located a 5 meters long broken capstone. It is named after a nearby "Chapelle de la Madeleine", which is still used.

Other Formation.

Manio Giant.

Near the Kerlascan alignment is located a single massive menhir, known as Giant. It is over 6 meters tall and was re-erected around 1900 by Zacharie La Rouzic.

Manio Giant

Megalithic Structures Worldwide

Practically, in the whole world are megalithic structures. It's impossible to describe them all. So, few examples will be dealt in following texts only.

Korean Peninsula.
Korean Peninsula has more megalithic dolmens than any other country in the world, which is around 40%, 30.000 – 50.000 or even more. Three of these sites were included in 2001 of the UNESCO list of World Heritage sites:

* **Kockang Dolmen Site** the largest and most diversified group in the village of Maesan. Many of them are located at altitudes of 15 – 50 meters along the southern foot of the hills that run east to west. The capstones are 1-5.8 meters long and weight 10 -300 tons. A total of 442 dolmens have been recorded.

* **Hwasun Dolmen Site** is located on the slopes of low ranges of hills, along the Chiseokgang River. The Hyosan-ri group comprises 158 structures and the Taesin-ri group 129. Many stones were taken away and can not be identified. This site was erected around 3.000 BC.

*__Kangwa Dolmen Site__ is located on the offshore island of Kangwa on the mountain slopes. The dolmans are higher than those on the other sites and appear to be older, especially, the dolmen at Bugun-ri (the largest dolmen; 7.1 by 5.5 meters) and Gochon-Ri.

Megalithic burial in Korea

Of course, three of the Korean dolmen sites have been described only, from around 30.000 or more, megalithic structures.

Megaliths in Turkey.

Why this jump from Korea to Turkey? Because Korea has the largest number of megalithic sites and in Turkey are the oldest megalithic structures. A large ceremonial complex was discovered at the top of a mountain ridge in the southeastern Anatolia Region of Turkey. Its age is astounding, the 9th millennium BC or even earlier. That was a time when the hundred thousand years glacial period ended. (The Ice Age is much longer time period) This site was before the agriculture was invented. It contradicts all, till now; accepted theories that people who lived during the hunter-gatherers could not have lived in villages. Also, Göbekli Tepe predates pottery, metallurgy and invention of wheel.

But who supervised the constructions? - An elite class of religious leaders controlled buildings and ceremonies that took place. If so, this would be the oldest known evidence for a priestly class.
Typical features of these megalithic structures are large circular constructions involving megalithic orthostats in sites Nevali Cori and Göbekli Tepe. At Göbekli Tepe four stone circles have been excavated from estimated 20. Some of them measure up to 30 meters across. Also, some stones have a variety of engraved pictures: human figures, boars, foxes, lions, birds, snakes and scorpions.
Less than 5% of the site have been excavated, the rest (95%) will be untouched to be explored by future generations (when techniques will have improved)

Göebleki Tepe excavation

Göebleki Tepe Pilar with bull, fox and crane in low relief

Middle Eastern Megaliths.

Practically in all Middle Eastern countries: Turkey, Syria, Yemen, Lebanon, Israel, Jordan, Saudi Arabia, Kharg Island in Iran and Barda Balka in Iraq, megalithic structure were found.

Under the sea in Israel at Atilt site, a semicircular arrangement of megaliths was found, dating around the 7th millennium BC.

Underwater Megalithic Structure in Atilit Site in Israel

The big numbers of dolmens are on both sides of the Jordan Rift Valley. Also, in the Golan Heights, the Hauran and in Jordan are the largest concentrations of dolmens in the Middle East. In Saudi Arabia, only few dolmens have been identified in the Hejaz.

Egyptian Megaliths.

700 kilometers south from modern-day Cairo is located in the desert, Nabta Playa, which once was a lake in the Nubian Desert. By the 5th millennium BC, the people in Nabta Playa had constructed the world's oldest megalithic astronomical calendar, 1000 years older, and similar to Stonehenge. This prehistoric calendar marks the summer solstice. Probably, the region was occupied only seasonally, only in summer when the local lake was filled with water for grazing cattle.

Also, in southwestern part of the Nubian Desert are other megalithic stone circles.

Nabta Desert Megalith

Behind this description of Egyptian megalith is a fascinating story. Obviously, the people who built these megalithic structures could not have lived in the desert. Around the 5th millennium BC, what is now desert, was savanna with lakes, trees and many animals and of course, human beings. However approximately during the 4 - 5 millennium BC the climate changed. Rain stopped and fertile land became sandy desert. All lakes, trees, shrubs and animals disappeared. Many human beings could not adapt themselves to the change and died. However, the survivors migrated east to the River Nile, where they found ideal condition: it was a paradise, River Nile with plenty of fishes, fertile land, and pasture for cattle, sheep and goats. On the Nile River they established a kingdom with a Pharaoh on its head. The time coincides, predynastic Egyptian civilization began around 3.500 BC and the people from the desert arrived to the Nile River around 4.000 BC. Around 2.500 BC the Egyptian civilizations was so advanced that they were building pyramids, the biggest and most famous structures in the world.

European Megaliths

The most common type of megalithic structures in Europe is the portal tomb – a chamber consisting of upright stones and with one or more large flat capstones forming a roof. Many contain human bones. They can be found in: Ireland, Galicia, Portugal, Sardinia, Netherlands, Germany, Denmark, and Wales. Most portal tombs were covered by earthen mounds.

Portal Tombs - Ireland

The second most common tomb type is the passage grave. It consists of square or circular or cruciform chamber with a slabbed or corbelled roof, with entrance by a long and straight passage. Originally portal tombs were covered by earthen mound. They can be found in: Ireland and France.

The third type of megalithic structures is gallery graves. These are axially arranged chambers placed under elongated mounds.
They can be found in: Ireland, England and Germany.

Still another type of megalithic structure is the single standing stone, or menhir. Some of them had an astronomical function or marker. In some places a long and complex alignment of theses stones exist.

In Italy dolmens are in: Apulia, Sardinia, Sicily, Palermo, Agrigento, Caltanissetta, Syracuse, and Ragusa, All structures were covered by a circular mound of earth, and dated to the early Bronze Age. In some of these dolmens the archeologists found numerous human bones and Early Bronze Age, ceramics.

Megalithic Structures in North America.
There are various megalithic structures in North America in: Massachusetts, New Hampshire, Vermont, Maine, Virginia, Ohio, Illinois, Connecticut, and in many more states. However the best known is the Mystery Hill.

Megalithic Structures in Mystery Hill.
The Mystery hill, also called America's Stonehenge is an archeological site consisting of a large number of large rocks and Megalithic stone structures scattered around on approximately 15 hectares. It is located within the town of Salem, New Hampshire in the northeastern part of United

States. It consist of a series of small stones, stone arrangements, underground chambers and one granite outcropping that has a rock structure built upon it and has been carved with groves.

Mystery Hill

A number of hypothesis exist as to the origin and purpose of these structures, however at the site are standing stones which were erected to align with astronomical events.

Many questions arise; why, when, and by whom these structures were erected.
All dates are uncorrected radio carbon years (BP) before present being defined as the year 1.950.
* Excavation in wall east of north stone by David Steward-Smith and Patricia Hume shows the date of 6.530 BP
* Fire pit at North Stone excavated by David Steward-Smith and Patricia Hume shows the date 3470 BP

* Flecks of charcoal lodged between the exterior stones of the north wall of the collapsed chamber 5 to 10centimeters above the bedrock shows the date 3475 BP
* Several units outside the north wall of collapsed chamber were found during excavation. At the 60 centimeters level charcoal was found with association with fire-burned stone spalls, hammer stone, broken pick and scrapper shows the date 2.995 BP.
* At the unit near the earthen ditch on the summit of the hill near the main complex of structures, charcoal was found in a seam of quarried bedrock, which shows the date 2.120 PB.
* In the parking lot for the visitor's center the remains of a North American lodge and multiple hearth features were found. Charcoal from different hearths produced three dates: 1910 to 190 BP.
* A Native American lodge hearth produced the date 1.640BP.
* A different Native American lodge hearth produced the date 1.195 BP

The BP dating is not reliable; however it shows that the whole complex of the Mystery Hill was built in stages and during many centuries. Probably the oldest monolithic structures are at least from 4.000 BC.

Also it's possible to deduce some dating from the fact that the Phoenician left some inscriptions on the stones. The late Barry Fell from the Harvard University claimed that he deciphered marking in: Ogham, Phoenician and Iberian script. So, the Mystery Hill must have been older than the arrival of the Phoenician, which could have happened around 1.000 BC.

At that time the Europeans did not yet arrived in North America, so all of these megalithic structures must have been erected by Native American.

Megalithic Structures in China.

Two types of megalithic structure exist in China: northeast type and the south type.

The Megalithic burials originated in northeast China, in particular in the Liao River basin, from where it spread into the Korean Peninsula. The earliest structures feature an above-ground burial chamber formed by heavy stones that form a rectangular cist. A big capstone is placed over the stone slab burial chamber, giving the appearance of a table-top. Some megalithic burials contain grave objects such as Liaoning bronze dagger. A number of archeologists think that these burials were graves of chiefs or prominent individuals.

Southern type megaliths are typically smaller than northeast megaliths. Southern megaliths have an underground burial chamber made of earth or lined with thin stone slabs. A massive capstone is placed on top and is supported by smaller stones. A small number of megalithic burials contain fine red-burnished pottery, bronze daggers, polished ground-stone daggers, and greenstone ornaments. Southern megalithic burials are often found in groups, spread out in lines that are parallel with the direction of streams. Also megalithic cemeteries contain burials that that are linked together by low stone platforms made from big river stones. Broken red-burnished pottery and charred wood found on these platforms indicate that these platforms were used for ceremonies and rituals.

Conclusion

Only few of tens of thousands Megalithic Structure was described in preceding texts and all of them were built by our ancestors, between 8.000 BC and 2.000 BC. Very little is known about them. What languages did they speak? How they lived? It can safely be assumed that they already practiced primitive agriculture. During the glacial period the cold climate hindered any attempt of planting and harvesting, cereals and vegetables. During this period they were obliged to pursue a nomadic, hunter-gathered lifestyle, following the animals they hunted. However, when the worldwide temperature increased our ancestor adapted themselves, very quickly, to new condition - agriculture. They changed their lifestyle from nomadic to sedentary. Agriculture is the world biggest invention and gave the Neolithic farmers free time, also the abundance of food. What effect this change had?

* With better nourishment the population started to grow rapidly. At the end of glacial period in the whole world lived about 1 million people, but after few hundred years it reached 3 or 4 million people.

* By having free time they pursued the biggest obsession of humankind, building. - In this case monolithic structures. (This obsession endures until today with the construction of: Pyramids, cathedrals, and now skyscrapers, highways, enormous sport stadiums, etc.)

* The sedentary lifestyle caused a social change. The religious leaders became tribal chiefs and decision takers. They planned and supervised the building of monolithic structures, which needed many thousands of day-workers to complete.

References

Encyclopedia Britannica.

Various Web pages.

Wikipedia.

FROM THE SAME AUTHOR

RELATOS Y LEYENDAS - Antigualas de Catamarca.
Spanish edition - 1984 - Club del Libro Cívico.

MY TRAVELS THROUGH CALCHAQUIES VALLEYS.
Bilingual edition - English & Spanish - 2005 – Elaleph.

THE COLLAPSE OF MODERN WAY OF LIFE
Bilingual edition - English & Spanish – 2006 – Elaleph.

WHO ARE THE JEWISH PEOPLE?
Bilingual edition - English & Spanish – 2007.

STORIES FROM MY LIFE.
Bilingual edition - English & Spanish - 2008 – Elaleph.

MYTHS AND FACTS.
English edition – 2010 - Lulu.com.

MISTERIOS DE LA MENTE
Spanish edición – 2010 - lulu.com

MYSTERIES OF THE MIND.
English edition – 2010 - Lulu.com.

PERSONAJE INOLVIDABLE.
Spanish edición – 2010 - Lulu.com.

RECUERDOS DE TIEMPOS DE ÑAUPA.
Spanish edition – 2011 - Lulu.com.

STORIES FROM BYGONE TIMES.
English edition – 2011 – Lulu.com.

THE COLLPSE OF WESTERN CIVILIZATION.
English edition – 2011 – Lulu.com.

WHO WAS IN AMERICA BEFORE COLUMBUS.
English edition – 2013 – Lulu.com.

THE STORY OF US.
English edition – 2013 – Lulu.com

MYSTERIES OF THE MIND
English edition – 2013 - Lulu.com.
Second edition.

INCREDIBLE CONNECTION.
English edition – 2013 – Lulu.com.

UNIVERSAL FLOOD.
English edition -2013 – Lulu.com.

www.ingramcontent.com/pod-product-compliance
Ingram Content Group UK Ltd.
Pitfield, Milton Keynes, MK11 3LW, UK
UKHW041914190726
13854UKWH00003B/1251

9 781304 646774